GW01464125

Syllables

Liam Black

For Siobhan

GUILDHALL PRESS

Acknowledgements

Our thanks to Manus Martin and the Training and Employment Agency for their continued support under the Action for Community Employment (ACE) Programme. Also to Derry City Council's Recreation and Leisure Department for providing generous Community Services Grant Aid which is greatly appreciated.

Special thanks to Danny Holmes and Tom McLaughlin.

© Guildhall Press   November 1994
ISBN 0 946451 29 X

Designed by Colin Darke and MC Design
Published by:
GUILDHALL PRESS
Community Book Publishers
41 Great James Street
Derry
BT48 7DF
Northern Ireland
Tel: (0504) 364413 Fax: (0504) 372949

Contents

Foreword	*4*
Syllables	5
Disinheritance	7
Inheritance	8
Gethsemane	9
They	11
The Last Rite	12
Siobhan	13
Black Death	14
Death of a 'Perhaps' Man	15
Looking Ahead	16
Close Relation	17
Granny's Warning	19
The Priest's Warning	20
Crossroads	21
Spider Spell	22
Razor	23
Mushrooming	24
What I Know	25
Absolute Dream	26
Divorcées	27
The 'Village'	28
The Cornflake Land	29
Marriage	36
Divorce	37
Derry Heir	38
Derry Air	39
Consuming	40

Foreword

It goes without saying that when we look for a definition, we choose one which is closest to articulating our own intuitive interpretation of the word or phrase in question. With poetry, I always go back to Samuel Taylor Coleridge: "Poetry is not the proper antithesis to prose, but to science. Poetry is opposed to science, and prose to meter... The proper immediate object of poetry is the communication of immediate pleasure... The best words in the best order."

By immediate pleasure, Coleridge does not mean that the poem's content is necessarily pleasant; but rather that the reader experiences a *frisson* of delight when encountering 'moments' which have the facility of acknowledging and exciting latent emotions. I experienced many such delights while reading Liam's poems and would heartily commend readers to give his best words *the best of order!*

Frank Galligan
Literary critic, poet and radio presenter.

Syllables

I, had not fathered hand casting shadowed
Head upon the wall. Mother's sound filled
My way showing me how to understand,
To study with bright eyes into the mind.

In infants, word was heard and played a game
With arm up high for permission to speak;
Sound became letter with word to follow
Pushing sound together on pencil line.

On high in each room the man from heaven
Touched us on the head, tummy and shoulders,
Set minds alight with wood and statue stares,
Mr Magic 'cause he was everywhere.

Break, lunch, home; time was on the clock behind
Always telling us to hurry, quickly;
In-between time was quiet time – no talk –
Just work at desk with pen and quiet thought.

Passed exam brought prize of brother's blazer
And new darkness donned in masculine form,
Eager agents of the man from heaven
Dressed in foreign vowel and living word.

Strange breed of solid desk-mate, country fed,
Orphaned off on terms of matronly care
Spoke with strange word, phonetic difference,
Yet more at home than: "Arms in the air, mate".

'*Ecce Romani*' was enjoyable,
'Native' tongue and foreign were learnt by head,
Heart was in the listening and saying;
Filter process to work, after bell's peal.

Depth was on the surface, easily read,
Learning was slow, exam oriented,
Too many questions, too many answers,
Release was in worded rescue with friends.

Rules, set in tradition and holy word,
Were everywhere, ready to be broken,
By souls tortured and shadowed by belief
Yet growing in self, with mind to follow.

Disinheritance

Granda hailed from hillside
Grassy, barn, hard,
Small field, big rock;

No gaze from big house
No hold of hired hand

No rise of spire
No sound of stolid bell.

Granda uprooted to city
Lights, hours, bustle,
Tall terrace, iron rail;

Bellow of gaffer returned
Time on Guildhall face

Multitude of spire
Gates to keep out.

Inheritance

Mother came from terrace
Allotment, dancing, polish,
Small hall, big hearth;

Corner shopping
Talk to neighbours

Cards on the table
Door on the latch.

Mother saw the suburbs
Roses, elocution, study,
Long driveway, oil-fired;

Supermarket food
Wave to neighbours

Monopoly on the table
Bell at the door.

Gethsemane

He was getting old
The past few years
And winter was on the way:
Mess and carpet to clean.

I roused him from his sleep
Into the sharp night
And back seat of the car
With three Digestive biscuits.

A few numbers down
Was our journey's end
As the vet's wife
Sent us round the back.

"What age is he?" came the vet,
As I dragged him from the car
Into the bright wee room;
"Fourteen," I proudly answered.

"Agh, the poor oul fella,
The poor oul fella,"
As he snipped some hair
From a front leg.

"See if you can get a vein."
"What?"
"You'll have to hold him, too."
It was a trap!

"Did you bring a bag?"
"What?"
"I'll get you one after."
My stare was frozen by syringe.

"Wait to see how quick this works."
I turned my head
And prayed my thumb was safe
Beside the needle.

As the vet straightened
I turned round and – Flop –
He sunk neatly to the floor.
"That was quick, wasn't it?"

He returned, tearing the top
Of an old potato bag,
Mud and dust inside:
The remains of something else.

We shoved him into the bag,
Tied the top well,
Lifted the dead weight out
And gently into the boot.

We did not stand on ceremony,
I paid my fiver
And left.
A job well done.

They

They mess you up and take you in
They make you eat their din,
They pick your mind and make you blind
They cloud your head with sin.

They speak of past to make it last
They like to hail their day,
They blend and change until they say
They knew no other way.

They curse at change and think it strange
They have no thought for shame,
They give advice to save from blame
They aim instead for gain.

They cook the system that they choose
They cannot risk to lose,
They aim to miss with every kiss
They can't confuse their views.

The Last Rite

We sat at night; each, alone, together;
And every night; witness outside your pain.
Helplessness; fear toward the end.

Passed off by hospital was sore,
I felt it whilst no other pain,
Watching your pain and hope-filled suffering.

When mother came into your room
And held your hand – sobbing – she hurt us all;
We felt truth in her tears.

Yet we laughed and played our childish game
As only we knew; and darkness grew
And nothing could we do except

Together,
Always together,
Ever together.

Siobhan

You sometimes worried
About older age
– Wrinkles, etc.,
And a declining shine –
This was unwarranted
You had no need for worry.

At nine and twenty years
You left your worries,
Your peerings for signs
Of deterioration without
Were transferred within.

Your beauty, your life,
Was leaving from within
And nothing could we do
'Cept wait, watch, worry.

Your smile stayed
And hope was ours
Until the end.

You loved life, happiness.
You loved.

Now, we are without you.

Black Death

I know death
I have met you
I don't like you
What you are
What you do.

You are nothing
You don't exist
Except in absence
In the nothingness
Of your being.

Death of a 'Perhaps' Man

His funeral
Came down Creggan Hill;
He had been shot
Through the head.

His body
Border-ditched
Blindfolded,
Hands tied behind back.

One bullet
Courtesy
Of a kangaroo
Court.

He must have told
The Koala bears
A big secret,
Perhaps.

Looking Ahead

The mother
Was very happy
When the fourth
One arrived.

A son, again.

"A shoulder
For each corner
Of my coffin,"
She confirmed.

Close Relation

Knelt, and said our prayers,
Sat an uncomfortable hour
Watching talk and tears
Pass by.

He looked great, a lot better
Than seldom recollection recalled
This, grandmother's brother;
A great-uncle, they say.

Too close for comfort, I say,
After half hour seated
At the foot of his coffin
And re-recountings of his death.

"The sore foot
And gangrene set in
And then the stroke
And him useless down one side."

Gangrene experts
—All the details fell out—
The blackened colour
That ghastly sight.

Suddenly, he was not dead,
My nostrils knew
The repugnant air
Of his weeping foot.

Still alive
Under the shroud
Was the foot
Of my close relation.

Granny's Warning

Give a man
Plenty
Of sex
If you want
To keep
His favours
At home;

Flavoured
Of course.

The Priest's Warning

Give your man
Plenty
To eat
At home
Or
He'll get hungry
When
He's out.

Crossroads

One night without the moon
We said hello vaguely;
A near neighbour my age
In different tribal wear.

We stopped where the short-cut
Meets the main road
And kissed wildly, kissed passionately,
Kissed blindly without the moon.

We walked together to the main road
Parted, said no goodbye
And have not spoken since;
Living lives beyond the moon.

Spider Spell

The spider now upon the wall
Is long of legs and body small,
Yet, so unlike the fly it kills
It takes its time and stays quite still;
No need has it of nervous flight
Never banging against the light
It casts its spell in a corner
Stops and waits like a sad mourner
Until chance causes it to pounce,
All legs embracing a fly lunch.

Razor

Be strong
Stand up
Head high
Don't take it
Stamp it out
Fight back
Hit hard
Knock down
And then,
Put the boot in.

Mushrooming

Early July, given light rain and heat,
Overnight dark heads would appear.
At first just one, a lonely silly walk
Head cranked, eyes scanning every inch;
Then a couple more, smiling profusely,
Leering through the recent bladed grass
Eyeing out another and another,
Then a whole soft fungal connection
Of earth's warts with umbrellas puffed over
To mask their latent poisonous intent.

Round to the rising bank above our pitch
They clamber, gorging themselves as they go
Until their eyes are full and down they fall
Backs to the ground, faces lifted skyward
Minds unlocated somewhere in between,
Mushrooming like little atomic clouds.

Toadstools and bad these were
When I was young and stamped
And kicked with plenty of gusto
And hands washed clean if touched;
But now, once off the ground, they do not rot
In the air, only in the minds of those
Gulled into wanting to catch a fairy or two.

What I Know

I know enough
To know
Enough
Is not enough
To know
To know
Enough to know.

Absolute Dream

Fantasy eyes
Smile with surprise
Reels of delight
Concentrate sight.

Touch of the hand
Magic command
Thoughts that persist
Cannot resist.

Fantasy thighs
Shelter surprise
Ready and waiting
Anticipating.

Divorcées

Prowling the night
With stealthy advances
Seeking out quarry
With warming glances
And smiles
That belie
Their true fancy.

They hunt in packs
Of threes and fours
Or a predacious pair,
The hunger in each
Sated only when one
Or other is fed.

The 'Village'

To suburbs of a misbegotten
Oasis of minds
Restless roads extend.

Fields around bare and bleak
Wet wind the only sound
Useless to the plough.

Lodgings locked in ports
Of Rush and Stewart,
Barnacle towns

That lodge their balance
With the weather's turn:
Tourist summer; student fall.

Pyramid in a desert,
Relay-post on the trail
This church and its graveyard.

The Cornflake Land

– At Home –

Humming a tune, tapping fingers on wheel
God, I nearly forgot to get more milk,
Glance at bus-stop, good, there's no-one I know
And could I have a bar of plain chocolate?

Neatly reverse Jap car into the drive
Wave blankly at neighbours, pick a few weeds,
Send children to collect their plastic toys
Tell dearly beloved who's changed their car.

Change your suit into cardigan and checks
Say grace for children before every meal,
Talk with knowledge about mortgage affairs
Always use plenty of tomato sauce.

Leave dearest to squeeze her fairy liquid
All the best pupils write with fountain pens,
Dust the garage, electric mow the lawn
Say silly words to the corner's new pram.

In the central heating sit in you chair
Admire your slippers and mother's knitting,
Watch nine o'clock news with Rich Tea biscuits
Wipe crumbs from your chest and onto the floor.

Correct the homework then it's question time.
Who forgot to practise their piano?
How well have all performed at school today?
And remember you are not to chew gum.

Make sure there's no dirt hidden behind ears
As you peck and pat their brushed hair goodnight
Sneakily smelling fresh mint from their mouths,
You notice them growing and feel so proud.

Resist the temptation of a late film
Time is better spent cycling with no wheels,
Three miles a day keeps our Flora man fit
Plus Saturday afternoon's golf, of course.

Bolt the doors and secure all the windows
We'll have three pints tomorrow if you please,
Undress in silence on your side of bed
Carefully folding your casual clothes.

I changed the linens again for you, dear
Those others were on for nearly two weeks;
Talk to mother of new washing machine
Then peck her on the cheek and turn to sleep.

Morning awakens with radio alarm
And curtain cord announces a new day,
Have a shower, dispose of another blade
Then lightly descend for cornflakes and toast.

After checking shoes polished, trousers creased,
Satchel the children off buswards to school,
Mirror inspect yourself, correct your tie,
Lip kiss dressing-gown goodbye at the door.

Curse quietly at traffic, pay to park,
Dust dandruff off in your rear-view mirror,
Trip into a shop for yesterday's news
After front glancing, fold under left arm.

Squeeze into the lift, release at fifth floor
Hurry along with fresh overheard joke
Retell to office who've heard it before,
Then turn to your corner as work begins.

Lunchtime laughter with penny conscious cards,
Filling sandwich – oh, it's different today –
Pour weak tea from flask into plastic cup,
Borrow some sugar, never sweet enough.

–On Holiday–

Months are taken in planning a fortnight
–We'll go back to Butlins again this year
It's cheaper, has lots the children enjoy,
For the second we'll go off on a tour.

First week is spent around roller rink's edge,
Watching firm bodies dive into the pool,
Three meals a day in communal sitting
Curtain colour change from the year before.

Pay extra one night for baby-sitter,
Chocolates and coke revive days of dating,
Leave before the end of the adult film
Unsure of the morals today on screen.

While wandering back step into a shade
Kiss and caress with passion arousing
Slip hand under blouse, feel passion arouse,
Rush back to chalet 'fore feeling wears off.

Pay extra to 'sitter – no time for talk
Strip clothes off in bundle at foot of bed
Quickly to business, mustn't make much noise,
Forget about caution this once, my dear.

Your father and I are tired, children
Go off and play for a couple of hours,
Don't go too far, we will be leaving soon
No, we cannot stay we booked for a week.

Travel for hours with pit-stops in lay-bys
Careful to stay well under speed limit,
Many songs are begun and town names told,
Mother's quiz book was worth it after all.

Never check into the first B and B
Remain in the car whilst mother inspects,
Beds are better linened in farmhouse parts
Food is not rationed, you can't spend a lot.

Wakening comes with a knock at the door,
Rise to the odour of sizzling bacon,
Wash with cold water in a metal bowl,
Memories of a thought to rise at dawn.

Eat your breakfast, you'll get nothing till lunch
This scone is lovely could we have some more,
Puncture your yolk to flavour a sausage
Look at the lovely hens outside, daddy.

Notice the bumps on the gravelly lane
The surer surface of the windy road,
Advice not enough – let me see the map,
You'd think they'd make roads a bit straighter.

A few more days to enjoy this free life
Breakfast at nine o'clock every morning,
Early to rise so that bathroom is free
And last down to the beach buys the ice-cream.

The water is lovely come on in, dear
Oh, leave your book you can read it tonight
The children are waiting – and bring the ball
Forget the oil, you don't tan anyway.

This is the place where that battle was won,
Stop the fighting and get down off the wall,
Would you look at your shoes they're thick with muck
Get into the car it's starting to rain.

Wipers wave their goodbye along the road
Silence in car 'cept for lack of sign-posts,
On arrival at home one day early
Good to be home, nothing like your own bed.

–At Christmas–

Only buy the cards with holy pictures
There's packets of ten at the Co-op store,
Get two packets, we've some left from last year
And while your there you'd better get more milk.

I really don't know where the money goes,
E. and T. bought us a present last year,
A bottle of sherry should be enough
They've not been the same since moving up there.

I've iced the cakes and the puddings are done
Shall we bother to light a coal fire, dear,
Mother sends her love, hope yours doesn't come
We all had enough of her grace last year.

Child-trailed procession down from the roof-space
Sees the Christmas tree unearthed yet again,
Potted once more in corner of front room
Strange how it seems to get smaller each year.

In the hall one morning appears the crib
Empty but for straw and unstable beasts,
Legs glued together in uncommon shapes,
Light at back always needs a new bulb.

The children watch with unshown amusement
How on selected days figures appear
– Let's hide the wise men, pretend they got lost,
– We'd better not, dad might cancel the show.

Sheets of Christmas carols are sneaked from school
Just in case correct words are forgotten,
As the different door bell rings set in tune
The merry songsters for a wrappings worth.

The largest socks long held ready for use
Suffer strong abuse when seen pinned to doors,
Look at the paintwork and holes in the wood
You have no respect at all any more.

Waited morning comes with sharp announcement
As small forms dive to bottom of the bed
Socks soon emptied of sweets and smaller toys,
Mustn't eat much or mother'll be annoyed.

Put all your new clothes on for mass today
And pay attention, don't stare at the crib,
You can open your presents after dinner
Now hurry up there's a lot to be done.

Crackers are pulled with predicted effect,
Jokes contained bring studies of amusement;
Father's paper crown never fits his head
Mother's tends to drop over her eyes.

Here, peel the Sellotape off at this end
Granny uses the best wrapping paper,
Isn't that lovely, let your father see
She really has you spoiled, you lucky ones.

Sweets eaten in parent-counted amounts
With soft centres left to the very end,
Games cast aside, attention on T.V.
– I hope we get staying up until the end.

Snow when it comes is too soon unwanted
Never enough to make a good snowman,
It is more like slush, leaves your feet soaking
Not like the snowy scenes on Christmas cards.

Holidays ending as T.V. changes
Back into its same old boring routine,
Go back to school to everyone's question:
And what did you get for Christmas this year?

Marriage

Mum and dad
Are getting married today

But not in church
Cause dad doesn't agree

And mum wants
A new T.V.

Anyway gran says
It's too late now

But dad just calls her
A silly old cow.

Divorce

Mum and dad
Are getting divorced today

I hope the judge
Won't blame me

I wanted a little
Brother you see

But mum and dad
Just couldn't agree

So I'll stay with
Gran for a while

Till mum calms down
And dad comes back

Down to earth.

Derry Heir

I sat,
And while you played
I aged

Watching stones and clay
Dislocate onto grass;

Sixteen month hands
On very important business.

A neighbourly cat
Prowled softly through
Unbroken bird din,

Suddenly
Shots split the air,
Made you run crying.

Cat melted
Into undergrowth,
Birds squawked louder
High in the trees

And, as sunlight
Slipped quickly
Into night,

Coldness
Gripped my chair.

Derry Air

Behind,
Smiles arose
With the sun

As we paid homage
To barbecue smoke
Raising the air

Through talk and din
And friends with children
Brightening the garden.

Suddenly a flying tadpole,
Propeller spun,
Manifested itself
In magnified form

Its hellish decibels
Drowning the moment.

Incensed,
We retreated quickly
Behind closed doors.

Consuming

Years ago
When I was young
People worked
And got enough
To do them;
They grumbled
And got on with it.

Years from now
When I'm older
People will wonder
How it all went
So badly wrong,
And people with it.